ARIES

ARIES

21 March–20 April

PATTY GREENALL & CAT JAVOR

MQP

Published by MQ Publications Limited
12 The Ivories
6–8 Northampton Street
London N1 2HY
Tel: 020 7359 2244
Fax: 020 7359 1616
Email: mail@mqpublications.com
Website: www.mqpublications.com

Copyright © MQ Publications Limited 2004
Text copyright © Patty Greenall & Cat Javor 2004

Illustrations: Gerry Baptist

ISBN: 1-84072-653-9

1 3 5 7 9 0 8 6 4 2

Printed in Italy

WHAT IS ASTROLOGY?

Astrology is the practice of interpreting the positions and movements of celestial bodies with regard to what they can tell us about life on Earth. In particular it is the study of the cycles of the Sun, Moon, and the planets of our solar system, and their journeys through the twelve signs of the zodiac— Aries, Taurus, Gemini, Cancer, Leo, Virgo, Libra, Scorpio, Sagittarius, Capricorn, Aquarius, and Pisces—all of which provide astrologers with a rich diversity of symbolic information and meaning.

Astrology has been labeled a science, an occult magical practice, a religion, and an art, yet it cannot be confined by any one of these descriptions. Perhaps the best way to describe it is as an evolving tradition.

Throughout the world, for as far back as history can inform us, people have been looking up at the skies and attaching stories and meanings to what they saw there. Neolithic peoples in Europe built huge stone structures such as Stonehenge in southern England in order to plot the cycles of the Sun and Moon, cycles that were so important to a fledgling agricultural society. There are star-lore traditions in the ancient cultures of India, China, South America, and Africa, and among the indigenous people of Australia. The ancient Egyptians plotted the rising of the star Sirius, which marked the annual flooding of the Nile, and in ancient Babylon, astronomer-priests would perform astral divination in the service of their king and country.

Since its early beginnings, astrology has grown, changed, and diversified into a huge body of knowledge that has been added to by many learned men and women throughout history. It has continued to evolve and become richer and more informative, despite periods when it went out of favor because of religious, scientific, and political beliefs.

Offering us a deeper knowledge of ourselves, a profound insight into what motivates, inspires, and, in some cases, hinders, our ability to be truly our authentic selves, astrology equips us better to make the choices and decisions that confront us daily. It is a wonderful tool, which can be applied to daily life and our understanding of the world around us.

The horoscope—or birth chart—is the primary tool of the astrologer and the position of the Sun, Moon, Mercury, Venus, Mars, Jupiter, Saturn,

Uranus, Neptune, and Pluto at the moment a person was born are all considered when one is drawn up. Each planet has its own domain, affinities, and energetic signature, and the aspects or relationships they form to each other when plotted on the horoscope reveal a fascinating array of information. The birth, or Sun, sign is the sign of the zodiac that the Sun was passing through at the time of birth. The energetic signature of the Sun is concerned with a person's sense of uniqueness and self-esteem. To be a vital and creative individual is a fundamental need, and a person's Sun sign represents how that need most happily manifests in that person. This is one of the most important factors taken into account by astrologers. Each of the twelve Sun signs has a myriad of ways in which it can express its core meaning. The more a person learns about their individual Sun sign, the more they can express their own unique identity.

ZO**DIAC** WHEEL

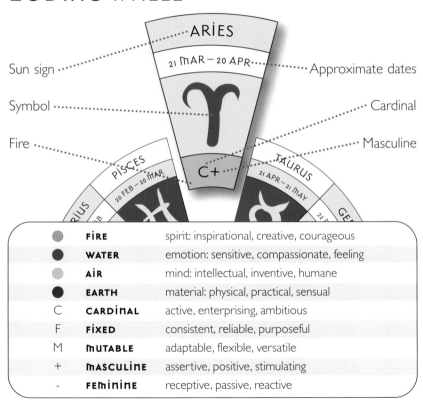

Sun sign

Symbol

Fire

ARIES

21 MAR – 20 APR

Approximate dates

Cardinal

Masculine

PISCES
20 FEB – 20 MAR

TAURUS
21 APR – 21 MAY

C+

🔴	**FIRE**	spirit: inspirational, creative, courageous
🔴	**WATER**	emotion: sensitive, compassionate, feeling
🟡	**AIR**	mind: intellectual, inventive, humane
⚫	**EARTH**	material: physical, practical, sensual
C	**CARDINAL**	active, enterprising, ambitious
F	**FIXED**	consistent, reliable, purposeful
M	**MUTABLE**	adaptable, flexible, versatile
+	**MASCULINE**	assertive, positive, stimulating
-	**FEMININE**	receptive, passive, reactive

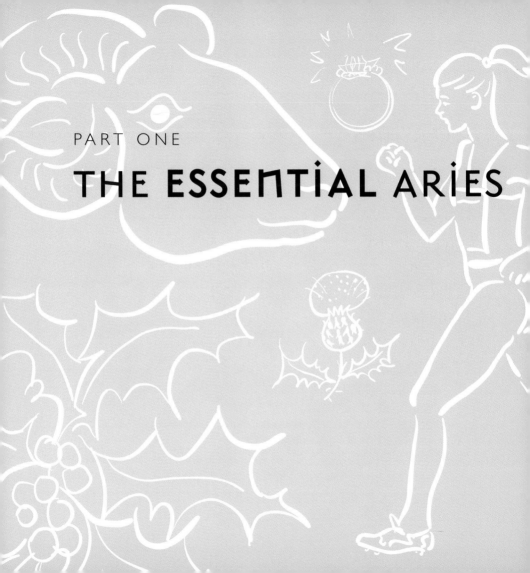

PART ONE

THE ESSENTIAL ARIES

RULERSHİPS

Aries is ruled by the planet Mars and is represented by the ram. There are earthly correspondences of everything in life for each of the Sun signs. Gemstones for Aries are diamond, ruby, carnelian, bloodstone, and red coral. Aries is a Masculine and Cardinal sign. Aries relates to the number one, the color red, the direction of east, and the metal iron, and it signifies action, adventure, pioneers, soldiers, surgeons, and welders, as well as hilly places, sandy places and new ground, holly, nettles, thistles, onions, garlic, mustard, radishes, and rhubarb. Running and sharp instruments are also part of the Aries domain.

ARİES

The part of the human body that
Aries represents is the head.

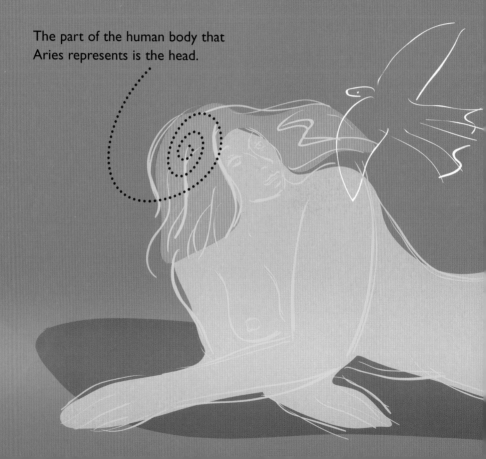

Diamond, ruby, carnelian

lily, nettles, thistles, garlic

surgeons, running

PERSO**O**NALITY

The astrological year begins with Aries at the Spring Equinox, when day and night are equal lengths. It marks the moment when the Sun starts to gain strength and the days grow longer. For this reason, Arians are known to be pioneering leaders, adventurers, and forward-looking individuals. Aries is the first sign of the zodiac, and the first of the three Fire signs, the others of which are Leo and Sagittarius. It is usually accepted that Arians will come first at everything, and they certainly expect to do so. Being ruled by energetic planet Mars, Arians love being challenged to compete, and throw themselves into the battle with enthusiastic delight, getting bored with anyone who gives less than their best. They have a strong sense of fair play and are rarely bad losers, not only because they usually win, but because, on those odd occasions when they do come second, they are the epitome of a good sport and are always the first to shake the winner's hand.

Aries represents strength and instinctive reactions. These admirable qualities are the basis for their daring and courage. The cosmic force imbues the animalistic Ram with procreative energy that overflows with life-giving force. Because they are so instinctive — they think faster than the speed of light — Arians are at their best when they are required to work to a deadline and under pressure of time, but they engage sincerely in any activity. They appear to be impulsive and headstrong, at times skipping the thought process by moving directly from inclination to action, but, in fact, they do think. They just do it faster than most people. The urgency to take action is sometimes so compelling for Arians that they don't pay much attention to potential pitfalls and often end up falling over themselves in order to achieve their objective. However, nobody is faster at picking themselves up, dusting themselves down, and renewing their effort, than an Aries.

Being the first Fire sign, Aries is like the primal fire that both creates and destroys. This enthusiastic quality enables Arians to initiate matters with ease. They're fast movers, but can become bored when the novelty has worn off. Arians are impetuous and energetic, like a child entering a playground full of new toys, but because of a tendency to act almost before thinking, they also have the ability to scrap an idea before it has been thought through. They are as spontaneous as a flash of lightning and usually their gut instinct points them in the right direction; however, they can be reckless because they tend to meet any challenge in life full on, rarely paying much attention to the consequences. They are brutally direct and honest, which can get them into trouble, but they would never back off from an argument. They also require that others are direct with them because subtle hints and suggestions usually fly past them like dust in the wind. They need people to be completely straightforward, and as open and direct as they themselves are.

Deception is not part of their nature: they lay all their cards on the table and fully expect the same of others. They have a strong imagination and can fantasize like no other but they couldn't lie to save their own life. If they try to bend the truth a little, they'll usually be as transparent as a pane of glass.

No party would be complete without the sunny presence of an Aries. They are full of the sort of vitality and spirit that keeps a crowd on its toes until well past the midnight hour. Quick-witted and happy-go-lucky, most Arians bring a breeze of hope and optimism into a room full of people.

Arians fall in love quickly, just as they would take up any new project. Their daring and direct manner offers hopeful suitors the possibility of a romance that's filled with adventure and excitement. They are courageous and energetic in their approach to life, so their partner will never have a dull moment, but a union with an Aries is definitely not for the faint-hearted.

Arians can be combative and confrontational, but never malicious. Their constant need to introduce new elements into any given situation makes it difficult for them to be satisfied with the present. They require challenge, excitement, and constant new thrills. In certain respects, they need taming and only those with enough malleability mixed with a strong sense of self in their nature would manage to endure a lasting relationship with the Ram. Since they get bored easily, the idea of going on a peaceful cruise in the Mediterranean would fill them with horror. Arians hate confinement and can become irritable and impatient if they don't have enough activity and sufficient novelty to satisfy their insatiable need for fresh ideas.

A rundown on Aries would not be complete without the word "selfishness" being included. It's a well-known Aries trait, but isn't the sort of selfishness that involves continually taking at someone else's expense. The tendency can be compared to the way an infant can only think of its immediate needs: not so that its mother will have less, but because the child is unable to be aware of the mother's needs. Arians also tend to lack modesty and tact. They get to the point fast, because they haven't time to waste, so for those used to gentler, more diplomatic ways of communicating, this can, at best, be rather unnerving and, at worst, offensive. They never mean to harm or insult: they just tell it like it is. They use the fastest, most direct route to communicate, so forget sugarcoated words and convoluted sentences. For this reason, when engaged in conversation with an Aries, it's important to say what you mean, to verbalize succinctly, and to keep the lines of communication open by listening as much as speaking.

Aries has a notoriously quick temper, which can be sparked into a raging inferno when provoked, but afterward amnesia sets in and all the hurts and insults are forgotten as quickly as they were aroused. Aries never holds a grudge and has little patience or understanding for anyone who dwells on the past or broods over an argument long after it should be considered forgotten.

The energetic, ambitious, self-centered, open, and honest individuals born under the sign of Aries are the epitome of "what you see is what you get," and they make no apologies for it. Why should they? They're terrific!

CAREER & MONEY

Arians work best when there's an element of competition present as this means they can employ the inexhaustible drive and initiative which are their trademarks. Arians enjoy being busy and dealing with one challenge after another, but they take exception at being ordered about and told what to do. It is possible to advise Arians or make a suggestion, but unless it's done in a purely informative way, they will simply ignore it all and continue to do things as they please. They have a strong sense of justice and can be sensitive when others come down hard on them. Ideally, Arians work independently, either through self-employment or by working in an environment where they are given a task to accomplish. You won't find many of this star sign cooped up in an office doing the daily nine-to-five grind. This would be akin to locking them in an insane asylum and eventually they'd begin to behave in a manner appropriate to such a place. Arians need open space and lots of room to stretch and be creative. And because Aries is ruled by Mars, they have no fear, know how to handle danger, and are fascinated by anything to do with fire or sharp objects. They do well in occupations involving the use of fire—their fascination with fire can be observed at summer barbecues!

Traditionally, they make fantastic butchers, welders, and smiths, but you'll also find many successful Arians working in pioneering fields, and being the first to reach a particular goal. Arians go where no man has gone before. They're the perfect people to be stuck on a deserted island with, for they would never go cold and hungry, or be short of things to do.

When it comes to money, Arians do not appear to be any different from your average individual, but they do have a particular style. They handle their finances either by quietly squirreling cash away, or by buying expensive transportable goods. They do all this discreetly and it would obviously not be appropriate to go and ask them about it, because they'll flatly deny it. That's not because they're secretive: it's simply not anyone else's business. They are not generally mean with money. In fact, if they can help out and it doesn't in any way infringe upon their own needs, they'll bend over backward for just about anyone and lend whatever they can spare. It's rare to find a spendthrift Aries, and if one is spotted spending large amounts of cash, it's likely that they have at least the same amount saved up. Reckless and foolhardy though Arians can look at times, make no mistake, they're quite sensible when it comes to cash and resources.

Added to that, they also seem to have luck at every stage of their career and in their financial lives because they're never afraid to take chances. Every endeavor is treated as something new. If it weren't, they wouldn't bother. Being the first sign of the zodiac, their enthusiasm and trust in life is refreshingly childlike, which is why they fear little and achieve much.

THE ARİES **CHİLD**

The assertive nature of Aries children is evident from the moment they come into the world. They are energetic, loud, and demanding in the way they express the desire to have their needs met. When it comes to learning how to move about under their own steam, they are impatient and likely to attempt to walk before they can crawl, and run before they can walk. It's a near-impossible task to hold an Aries child back. They will rush head-first into any activity that draws their attention, which often has their parents watching them continuously. Here is a child who truly does "get into everything." But this wonderful enthusiasm has a downside; besides being tiring for those trying to keep up with them, it often leads to the young Arians having scraped knees, stubbed toes, and perhaps even breaking the odd bit of crockery as they attempt to do everything, and now! But Arians are highly resilient and quickly bounce back, throwing themselves at a new and exciting activity as soon as they have recharged their batteries.

The Aries child is competitive and does well in both the academic and sporting arenas of school life. They enjoy the position of being first and will naturally do all they can to ensure that others don't get too far ahead of them. Natural born leaders, Arians are adept at encouraging their peers to get involved in adventurous activities and they often take their playmates to the point of exhaustion. As Aries children grow into adolescence, the self-centered and demanding aspects of their nature can become more prominent if they haven't been taught the value of give and take earlier on in life. However, provided they're made aware that every individual has as much right to achieve their goals as they have, young Arians are exciting and inspiring people to have around.

PERFECT GIFTS

Remembering that Arians get bored easily and have an insatiable desire for all things new and interesting, a novelty item for the Aries friend or loved one will always strike a chord. The "latest thing" will amuse and fascinate, but it had better be fresh off the production line and truly cutting edge or else they've probably already seen it, and done it. Preferably, a gift will be something that holds their interest for longer than five minutes, but this could be a tall order. Keeping in mind that Aries is ruled by passionate Mars, anything racy, sexy, and sparkling will completely delight their excitable temperament. They like bold colors and things that make a strong statement, so if you are considering traditional gifts such as socks, ties, or toiletries, make sure that they're chosen from the latest designer ranges. Bearing in mind Aries' connection with the head, headwear is a good choice of gift but make it stylish and simple because Arians are naturally hot-blooded creatures and the wrong sort of hat might end up spending more time on a shelf. Toys and gadgets will certainly make them smile but don't forget the batteries—Arians will want to play with their gifts right away.

FAVORITE FOODS

Arians will try anything … once! That includes food, but once a decision has been made as to whether they like something or not, they'll stick to that decision unless somebody can come up with a very good reason why they shouldn't—which is unlikely. If they liked something as a child, then Arians will probably continue to like it into adulthood. Simple foods that provide all the necessary nutritional components to sustain a highly energetic lifestyle are therefore definitely "on the menu."

The busy Aries is prone to eating on the run but a concerted effort should be made to avoid it. So for breakfast, cereals, perhaps with some fresh fruit or fruit juice, are the best start to the day. They are unlikely to want a full cooked breakfast but might be tempted by a bacon sandwich to go. If morning tea, or more likely coffee, is on the agenda, then Arians will take a minimum of two cookies to accompany it, but later on they will feel that they really should have some fresh, perhaps even raw, vegetables to make up for the earlier indulgence. Due to the active mental energy of Arians, brain food such as fresh fish is highly recommended. Being a Fire sign, they do like hot food, but too many spices that confuse the taste buds or mask the natural flavors of the food are unlikely to please their palate.

FASHİ☉∏ & **STYLE**

When it comes to clothes, anything that is fussy or restricts the movement of the body just for the sake of being fashionable will definitely be rejected and flung onto the charity shop pile by Madame or Monsieur Aries. That doesn't mean that Arians aren't stylish; they like to make a strong impact and will wear the latest in cutting-edge trainers, sportswear, and casual clothes. But they will just as happily smarten up in classic line suits, well cut to fit the body, when the occasion demands.

"Ready to wear" best describes the Aries fashion preference and "simplicity" is their watchword. Both the male and female born under this sign are happiest and look most confident when attired in modern classics like designer blue jeans and a T-shirt.

When choosing accessories, every Aries should go straight to the milliner because most hats will flatter them. Another must-have item is a good pair of sunglasses, while just a single piece of jewelry—a diamond-encrusted watch, for example — is all that's required to set off any favorite outfit.

Arians look good in strong colors, particularly red, black, and white, or an eye-catching combination of all three. If they absolutely can't avoid patterned fabric, then bold geometric shapes or sedate stripes are preferred. Nothing flouncy, frilly, or flowery will appeal to the direct and assertive Aries clotheshorse. It's always easy to recognize Arians by their no-nonsense, simple, classic style, whether they're headed out for a run or off to a ball.

İDEAL **HOMES**

Being in an Aries home is a truly fascinating experience. It doesn't matter where that home is as long as it has loads of space and easy access to civilization and action. A large metropolitan home filled with gadgets and gizmos would be the Aries ideal. They need lots to play with in order to keep their interest constantly stimulated, but the pile-up of discarded items that are no longer of interest could get in the way. Organization is not their forte. However, walking into an Aries home, with its vast array of things, is an amazing encounter that can leave some folk a little exhausted. The Aries home does offer a high degree of comfort. They're not fussy about guests coming in with their shoes on, making themselves at home and sitting where they like. There's a considerable amount of pride attached to an Aries abode and they want people to feel at home, but their idea of the perfect pad isn't everyone's. It's best to keep all criticisms hush, and to appreciate the eclectic qualities of a home belonging to someone who is obviously very busy.

PART TWO

RISING SIGNS

WHAT IS A **RISING** SIGN?

Your rising sign is the zodiacal sign that could be seen rising on the eastern horizon at the time and place of your birth. Each sign takes about two and a half hours to rise — approximately one degree every four minutes. Because it is so fast moving, the rising sign represents a very personal part of the horoscope, so even if two people were born on the same day and year as one another, their different rising signs will make them very different people.

It is easier to understand the rising sign when the entire birth chart is seen as a circular map of the heavens. Imagine the rising sign — or ascendant — at the eastern point of the circle. Opposite is where the Sun sets — the descendant. The top of the chart is the part of the sky that is above, where the Sun reaches at midday, and the bottom of the chart is below, where the Sun would be at midnight. These four points divide the circle, or birth chart, into four. Those quadrants are then each divided into three, making a total of twelve, known as houses, each of which represents a certain aspect of life. Your rising sign corresponds to the first house and establishes which sign of the zodiac occupied each of the other eleven houses when you were born.

All of which makes people astrologically different from one another; not all Arians are alike! The rising sign generally indicates what a person looks like. For instance, people with Leo, the sign of kings, rising, probably walk with a noble air and find that people often treat them like royalty. Those that have Pisces rising frequently have soft and sensitive looks and they might find that people are forever pouring their hearts out to them.

The rising sign is a very important part of the entire birth chart and should be considered in combination with the Sun sign and all the other planets!

THE RISING SIGNS FOR ARIES

To work out your rising sign, you need to know your exact time of birth—if hospital records aren't available, try asking your family and friends. Now turn to the tables on pages 38–43. There are three tables, covering New York, Sydney, and London, all set to Greenwich Mean Time. Choose the correct table for your place of birth and, if necessary, add or subtract the number of hours difference from GMT (for example, Sydney is approximately ten hours ahead, so you need to subtract ten hours from your time of birth). Then use a ruler to carefully find the point where your GMT time of birth meets your date of birth—this point indicates your rising sign.

ARIES WITH ARIES RISING

One hundred percent pure hero! The person born with the Sun in Aries and Aries rising is a courageous pioneer blazing a path for the rest of the world to follow. They have the self-confidence to start up any enterprise without the slightest thought for unforeseen difficulties, and if they are faced with having to jump through burning hoops, they do it with the same vigor and enthusiasm as they do everything else. They express their thoughts and feelings vehemently and with inspirational passion. "Double" Aries personalities are ambitious and must have their own way. They expect to be the leaders in every situation, which could present problems when someone else comes along who also wants to be in charge. It wouldn't be uncommon to find this Ram with horns locked in a duel. However, once the dust has settled, these Arians will pick up right where they left off and, with luck on their side, will keep pushing toward each and every new horizon.

ARiES WiTH **TAURUS** RiSiNG

The fiery, impulsive aspects of the Aries nature are less obvious when earthy Taurus is rising. These individuals appear less excitable, more steady, and generally a whole heap more cautious. Taurus softens some of the impetuous, abrasive Aries qualities, giving a gentler, mellower feel to the outward demeanor. These people have a love of luxury and, given the chance, they'll be more than happy to while away the hours relaxing in an aromatherapy bath, or being squeezed and stroked on a masseur's table while they dream up their next brave move to conquer the world. Any attempt to get them to skip the pampering that is part of their daily ritual will be met with intransigent refusal. They need to be left to their own devices, they need to do things their own way and no other, and they will. While still being an ambitious and enterprising Aries, having Taurus rising adds a degree of determination and consistency to their efforts, making it easier for them to carry projects through to a conclusion. The hot-headed Aries temper is still there, but with Taurus rising it is less easy to provoke and much slower to reach critical mass. However, when it is provoked, the strength of the blast will be devastating.

ARIES WITH **GEMINI** RISING

The active, energetic, and ambitious Aries personality can add ingenuity, wit, and a versatile intellect to its list of strengths when Gemini is rising. Expressing themselves verbally is an absolute imperative. This person could start a conversation in an empty room and, what's more, it would be fascinating! They still have a passionate quest for adventure but the pursuit of knowledge is first and foremost in their mind, which is why they gather friendships like a philatelist collects stamps. They have at least one contact for each of their interests and they'll have plenty of different groups of people to choose from when they need to have a good chat. They like variety, they talk nonstop, and they require lots of stimulation. It's almost impossible to get them to sit still for longer than five minutes. As a result, they are highly productive individuals and are capable of achieving much, as long as they are also able to channel their interests and efforts. These individuals can appear very highly strung and if the constant need for fresh intellectual input is not satisfied, then the Aries with Gemini rising may become nervous, irritable, and incredibly argumentative for want of something exciting to engage in.

ARiES WiTH **CAПCER** RiSiПG

♋ All the passion and enthusiasm of Aries gets a powerful emotional input when Cancer is the rising sign. This is an incredibly strong combination, bringing to the ambitious Aries personality the added qualities of an excellent imagination and finely tuned instincts. Outwardly, this Aries is more sympathetic, sensitive, understanding, and kind, and is very adept at building feelings of trust and familiarity in others. But make no mistake, they are still the fiery, impulsive, and often impatient person that Aries is known for. It's just that the edges are slightly softer—except when it comes to defending loved ones. The mixture of Aries with Cancer rising produces a ferociously protective individual. No one of sane mind would dare tread on the toes of this animal. Being completely unapologetic for their desire for respect, status, and the good things in life, Arians with Cancer rising make terribly industrious and diligent individuals. Because they also seem to have an uncanny knack for knowing what it is that excites the interest and imagination of others, they often find themselves living life in the public eye.

ARiES WiTH **LEO** RiSiПG

♌ Beautifully bold, courageous, and noble. How Arians with Leo rising cut a dashing figure that deserves all the admiration they receive! Big-hearted, philosophical, and with a commanding presence, they inspire faith and loyalty in all who find themselves on the receiving end of their extravagant generosity. Boy, do these individuals know how to make friends and influence people! The self-starting, energetic Aries becomes even more passionate when Leo is rising, and the need for freedom and adventure is heightened. However, should anybody wound their pride or not show appreciation, well, the pain this would cause may result in the offender suffering banishment at best, obliteration by hellfire and brimstone at worst. Flattery is the best way to get around Arians with Leo rising. They're reasonable and will listen to advice as long as it's not forced upon them. They'll dismiss anyone who tries to issue an order, but will graciously accept comments, compliments, or even criticism, as long as they are expressed in flowery, sweet sentences. The rewards of being associated with this individual are great but so are the demands — unless treading carefully comes naturally to you.

ARIES WITH **VIRGO** RISING

♍ A sharp, penetrating, and shrewd mind is the result when the Aries individual gets Virgo rising. This is the ultimate combination for a quick learner, and Arians are very fond of study. Arians with Virgo rising are methodical in their approach to the constant stream of activities they willingly undertake, and once they get going, their concentration is hard to break. For Arians, having Virgo rising adds a very rigorous quality to their array of valuable attributes. The bold and impetuous Aries nature becomes more conservative and prudent, while the legendary Aries self-confidence is less assured and more modest, with a definite air of vulnerability, which makes these Arians incredibly attractive to the opposite sex. Lacking in drive, determination, and self-control they are not and there is definite evidence of physical endurance, as can be witnessed by anybody seeing the Aries with Virgo rising in the gym! In business and financial affairs, they are extremely clever and diligent, and although they may appear to be shy and understated on the outside, their inner resources hold a vast potential for growth, transformation, and success. This is a winning combination!

ARIES WITH **LIBRA** RISING

This combination produces an Aries who is as accommodating as Aries can get. An Aries with Libra rising is the ideal PR person — not shy about meeting and greeting people, pleasant to look at and to spend time with, and able to corral people into signing on the dotted line. Once they have what they want, however, these Arians will be off like a shot to the next conquest. They enjoy flitting from one thing to another, from admirers to appointments to parties. They seek attention and they find it. When the energetic, rough-and-ready enthusiasm of Aries is focused through the refined lens of Libra, with its diplomacy and cheerful geniality, the result is a totally irresistible person. The epitome of good taste and style, these Arians enjoy the finer things in life and are drawn to the artistic, musical, and literary. However, the normally decisive action of Aries now seems to be slightly less sure of itself because it needs some peace and harmony. With Libra rising, Aries is less selfish and is superb at learning what brings happiness to others.

ARiES WiTH **SCORPiO** RiSiNG

♏ On the outside, the Aries with Scorpio rising is attractive and sexy, and seems to be shy, quiet, and unassuming. But try to stroke it and it will soon become apparent that this ain't no fluffy toy. These are artful, brooding, clever individuals who make the perfect allies for deserving friends or lovers, but cross the line and you would be lucky to live to regret it! Arians with Scorpio rising may sometimes appear to be the ultimate control freaks. They're completely self-assured and stubbornly believe they know the best method for handling everybody's situation. However, should someone need their help to sort out a problem, they won't rest in their diligence and support until the problem no longer exists. With Scorpio rising, Arians are much more covert in the methods they use to get their own way. Still as honest as the day is long, they are perhaps a little more secretive and subtle about achieving their aims. Aries and Scorpio are both very energetic signs, Aries in an outward manner and Scorpio inwardly. The combination of the two makes a powerful individual who will stop at nothing to achieve perfection and complete success.

ARiES WiTH **SAGiTTARiUS** RiSiNG

↗ This Aries knows how to enjoy life. With Sagittarius rising, there is never a dull moment and it would be easy to believe that they take nothing seriously and are simply out to have a good time. This is partly true and it would be just like them to pontificate extensively on the advantages of taking nothing seriously in life except having a good time. How do they manage? They are incredibly creative, resilient, and youthful individuals who don't know the meaning of discouragement. Problems simply aren't a big deal for they keep going no matter what. When they meet with a brick wall, they find a way of blasting through it or climbing over. Like children, they never take "no" for an answer and always get what they want. The Aries with Sagittarius rising appears to be the ultimate free spirit. They can't abide being cooped up or having their independence threatened, and they're usually very lucky, mainly due to an unflagging optimism. Incredibly opportunistic, they never miss a chance to take advantage of any situation that offers adventure and excitement. Even-tempered, big-hearted, and good-natured, they're so attractive to almost everyone they meet, they'll never lack for friends, all of whom are longing to be part of their wonderful world.

ARiES WiTH **CAPRiCORN** RisiNG

This might be the one kind of Aries who ends up following in their father's footsteps, and they'll either do it grudgingly or they'll do it and then some. Give Aries with Capricorn rising something to live up to and they'll certainly get up to living it. This is a very sensible person, one who combines the powers of youth with the wisdom of age at every point in life. When young, they seem to be old, and when old, they seem young. They are ambitious, competitive, and successful. In fact, no mountain is too high. They need constant challenges if they are to feel alive. Starting from the bottom and working up holds no fears for them because they know that with hard work and determination, they can achieve anything. Arians with Capricorn rising are a dynamic combination that exudes a powerful animal magnetism and intense sexuality, making them terribly attractive, even though they often seem completely unaware of it. If it occurred to them to use this irresistible quality in the pursuit of achieving their aims, then the effect they could have on the world and on the people around them would be profound.

ARİES WİTH **AQUARİUS** RİSİɳG

Friendly, helpful, and interested, this Aries could stay up all night long chatting with a friend about the different choices that that friend is faced with, whether concerning career, relationship, or family issues. They will immerse themselves in the topic and make just the right suggestions. They communicate and comprehend everything and anything, which is why they are capable of forward thinking and objectivity. Yes! Individuals with the Sun in Aries and Aquarius rising are inventors and innovators *extraordinaires*. The constant stream of new ideas that issue forth from the mouths of Arians with Aquarius rising may seem radical and way out, but these individuals are no "space-cadets." Their logic has an inspirational quality but it is also fundamentally practical. They want to revolutionize the world and make it a more humane place for everybody, and what's more, they won't ever stop trying. They have razor-sharp intellects and photographic memories, and their taste inclines them toward high cultural pursuits such as philosophy, art, and literature. However, the realm of emotions is completely foreign to these Arians. They can understand feelings in a rather remote kind of way but have very little interest in discussing them. People feel feelings, they don't talk about them!

ARIES WITH **PISCES** RISING

Normally with Aries, everything is on the table, but with Pisces rising, a lot goes unsaid and unseen. It's not that they have anything to hide, just that they don't see a good reason to reveal all, particularly when it comes to money. Finances and self-worth are no doubt big issues but the only person they'll ever share those private details with is the person that they feel at one with — the emphasis being on the word "person" rather than "people." Arians with Pisces rising are amiable and sweet but compared with other Arians, they prefer to spend time in more intimate surroundings. Put them in a wild, raucous party and they'll certainly blend in and have a great time, but they'll also vanish without trace when they've decided they've had enough. Pisces rising gives the self-interested Arians a more empathic, sympathetic aspect to their nature. They appear to be less pushy, more courteous, and modest. All the Aries fire and willful ambition is still there but it's softer, gentler, and less obvious when projected out into the world through the watery sign of Pisces. This is what gives these Arians that seductive and intriguing appeal.

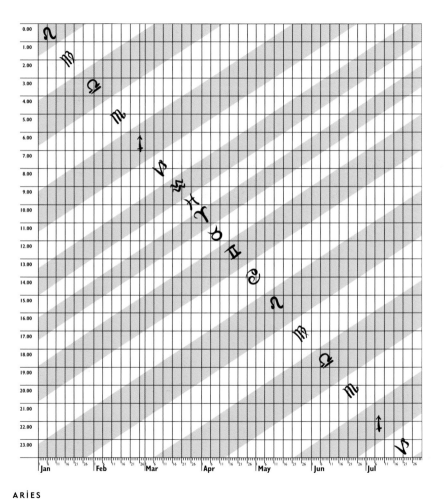

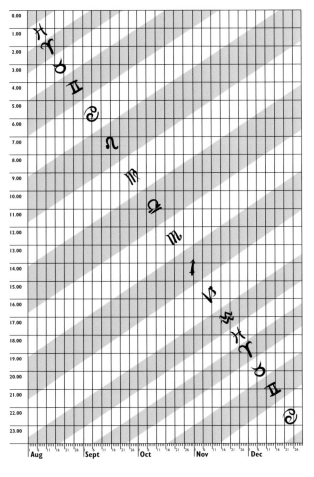

RISING SIGN
TABLE

New York

latitude 39N00
meridian 75W00

♈	aries	♎	libra
♉	taurus	♏	scorpio
♊	gemini	♐	sagittarius
♋	cancer	♑	capricorn
♌	leo	♒	aquarius
♍	virgo	♓	pisces

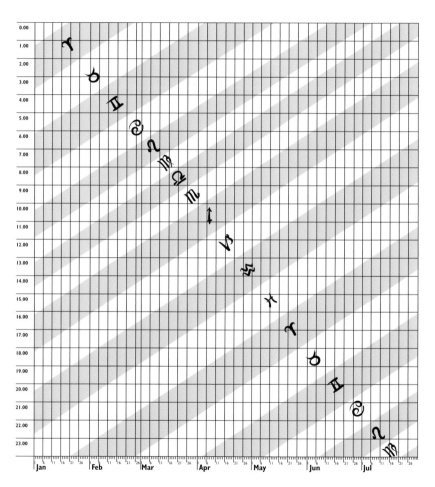

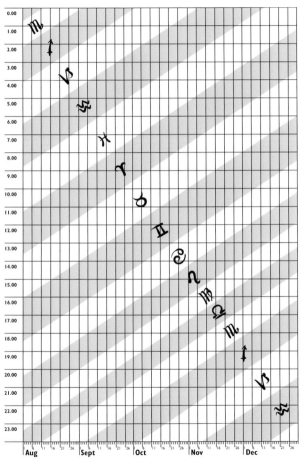

RISING SIGN
TABLE

Sydney
latitude 34S00
meridian 150E00

♈ aries   ♎ libra

♉ taurus   ♏ scorpio

♊ gemini   ♐ sagittarius

♋ cancer   ♑ capricorn

♌ leo   ♒ aquarius

♍ virgo   ♓ pisces

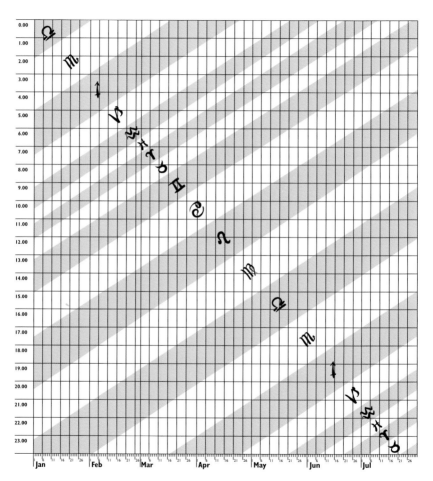

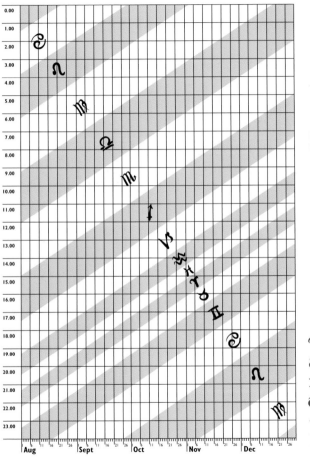

rising sign
TABLE

London

latitude 51N30
meridian 0W00

Υ aries Ω libra

$\bigvee$ taurus $\mathbb{M}$ scorpio

$\mathbb{I}$ gemini $\nearrow$ sagittarius

$\mathfrak{S}$ cancer $V\!\!\!S$ capricorn

$\mathfrak{N}$ leo $\aleph\!\!\!\aleph$ aquarius

$\mathbb{M}$ virgo $\mathcal{H}$ pisces

PART THREE

RELATIONSHIPS

THE ARİES **FRİEɳD**

The open, honest, and direct nature of Arians makes them willing and energetic friends. They approach all new acquaintances with a refreshing audacity which is as disarming as it is attractive. Always looking people straight in the eye and showing genuine interest in potential new friends, they smile easily and engage enthusiastically in any topic of conversation, even if they know very little about it!

Arians are completely at ease when expressing what they think, and because they are bold and opinionated they sometimes get themselves into heated debates, putting across their point of view with a ferocity that has other, less confident, types backing away to safety.

Nobody gets off lightly with an Aries as their pal! They'll be told exactly when their behavior is unacceptable or when their thinking is too fluffy for the Ram's taste.

When Arians are challenged, they engage fully in the battle, exchanging many tactless remarks and occasionally displaying their hot-headed temper in all its full, flaring glory. They demonstrate a childlike enjoyment of the verbal sparring and whether they win or lose, they bear no grudges. When it's over, Arians will easily forget any transgressions, shake hands firmly, and call their opponent "friend."

ARİES WİTH **ARİES**

Shared enthusiasm can be a real treat! No one could bring these two down when they get together and there is no stopping a couple of Rams on a mission. They encourage each other to join in a circus of laughter, fun, and adventure—until there's cause for disagreement. With both being so single-minded, when there's a bone of contention between them, it's impossible for either to see the other's point of view. Neither is going to wave a white flag and surrender, so unless they can agree to disagree, time spent together should be limited to short but happy bursts.

ARİES WİTH **TAURUS**

Aries is naturally drawn to the kindness and understanding that seems to ooze from the pores of Taurus and Taurus can't help but be curious and entertained by the lively energy of Aries. Although Aries will be straight in there with a smile, forming a friendship without a second's hesitation, Taurus is a little more cautious, at least in the beginning. Taurus likes to pace the journey while Aries runs on full throttle. But both indulge passionately in whatever interests them and if they find a subject that is mutually intriguing, then this is the perfect combination for developing a lasting, loyal bond and friendship. Sometimes exciting, always steady.

ARIES WITH GEMINI

These two are both talkative, witty, and restless. There's always an atmosphere of fun and adventure even if they're only spending the evening in front of the television. Aries delights in the clever, fast-moving intellect of Gemini, while Gemini eagerly gets caught up in the enthusiasm of the fearless Aries. However, when two such high-energy people are together, the excitement has a tendency to spiral out of control. Both are thrill-seekers, neither wanting to miss out on a moment's fun, so exhaustion could be a frequent result of time spent together. Great playmates they may be, but they need time apart to recharge their batteries.

ARIES WITH CANCER

Both Aries and Cancer are Cardinal signs, which means that both are dependable and very able, especially in situations where someone needs to take charge. Together they can conquer the world—as long as they can agree ahead of time on who is going to do what. There will be moments when the sensitive Cancer will feel hurt and dismay at being on the receiving end of the tactless hot-tempered Aries tongue, just as Aries will lose patience with having to constantly watch what is said around the Cancer who is prone to tearful, emotional outbursts. But when the chips are down, neither could want for a better champion than the other.

ARiES WiTH **LEO**

♌ Ideas and inspiration gush forth from these two minds like a geyser. Together, they're never bored, never at a loose end. There's always something Aries and Leo will find to do. These two Fire signs immediately respond to the spark of friendship. The inspirational qualities of Aries meet their perfect partner in the creativity of Leo. Once they find a common interest, they're off like a rocket, but if there's a hint of disagreement, a clash of egos could send their fires raging out of control. As long as they're both willing to admit to the possibility of competition, they should be able to cope with it with good-natured cheer.

ARiES WiTH **ViRGO**

♍ It's difficult for Aries and Virgo to see eye to eye. For the most part, they're running at different speeds. Arians wants to get where they're going fast, paying little attention to the finer details. Those finer details, however, are what intrigues Virgo so much — the intricate subtleties of organization and efficiency, practice and preparation. One has no patience at all; the other has the patience of a saint. Inevitably there will be points where they meet — their mutual respect for one thing — but even when they like each other and are fully engaged in some mutual interest, they'll find this friendship incredibly hard work.

ARIES WITH **LIBRA**

As opposite signs of the zodiac, these two are definitely attracted to one another, but their friendship may be difficult to define because they both like to push against the boundaries. They could get so drawn into each other's company that they end up excluding all other people, including other potential intimates. They have a natural ability to get each other into an excited, exuberant, wound-up state because they're both so restless. But they'll complement each other well in most situations, particularly when playing "good cop/bad cop." The phrase "bosom buddies" springs to mind with Aries and Libra.

ARIES WITH **SCORPIO**

Aries and Scorpio can work very well together when they have an objective in mind. Aries likes a mission and Scorpio always has an agenda, so as a team, they are formidable and unconquerable. Both have unstoppable energy and a passionate drive, however, if they're left to drift without an aim, their friendship could prove to be less than compatible because they're fundamentally very different. Aries is all about action, impulsiveness, and spontaneity where Scorpio is all about deep thought, deliberation, and intensity. In small doses, anyone can tolerate anyone, however, this pairing is more repelling than compelling.

ARIES WITH **SAGITTARIUS**

These two Fire signs get on like a house on fire but their raucous slapstick behavior could wear down the tolerance of friends and family alike so they'll need to tone things down if they want to keep their other friends. Aries and Sagittarius are like-minded yet Sagittarius can enhance the spiritual awareness of Aries, and Aries never fails to stimulate the inquiring Sagittarius mind. It's all action, energy, and enterprise when these two are together. Like children, they can play for hours on end and get up to all sorts of mischief. If tempers flare, sparks and flames will fly, but they're both quick to forgive.

ARIES WITH **CAPRICORN**

There's something unmistakable in the atmosphere when Aries and Capricorn meet but maybe it's not really desirable to have a Ram and a Mountain Goat charging at one another! They both want to be leader, which could create problems, so they each need to curb their self-centeredness in order to get along. Capricorns need to loosen up their apprehensive, even pessimistic tendencies, while Arians need to stabilize their impulsive, headstrong dispositions. There is a sense of excitement when they're together, as if something really big is about to happen, and more often than not, something very special does.

ARiES WiTH **AQUARiUS**

Intellectually, Aquarius stimulates and inspires Aries' hungry appetite for life. Neither of these two signs will ever be at a loss for something to do or think about. They are capable of really sparking one another off and life feels more exciting when they are in each other's company. There's an exuberant energy in a room when Aries and Aquarius are together, and they both feel very alive. However, Aquarians can be stubborn and, once decided on something, they stick to it, while Arians, infuriatingly, can get sidetracked and will move onto bigger and better things if they get the urge.

ARiES WiTH **PiSCES**

Aries has a limited attention span while Pisces has a limited amount of bubbly energy. After a while, Pisces can seem moody but really it's because they need to be alone to recharge their batteries. Aries can easily hurt Pisces' feelings, whereas Pisces can be over-accommodating to Aries. All in all, Aries needs to be more sensitive and Pisces less so. Because Pisces and Aries are next to one another in the zodiac, it's likely that each has planets in the sign of the other, and if this is the case, they'll have more in common than is immediately apparent.

THE **ARİES WOMAN** İN LOVE

She's passionate, feisty, and completely unstoppable when she's made up her mind to win a particular lover. This girl knows her own mind, feels the urgings of her spirit and goes with it—one hundred percent! The Aries girl will never be in a state of doubt, unsure of her feelings, or wondering whether this is "the one!" Her attitude to relationships is "love 'em or leave 'em!" If it's love, she'll pull out all the stops to make it work; if not, then she'll move on. For this reason, the Aries girl is totally comfortable with not being attached. She's too busy to mess about. If there's ever to be a chance that a romance will develop into something more lasting, she needs to be head over heels in love, thinking about her lover last thing at night and first thing in the morning. She would rather be on her own, sexy and single, than go through the motions of being in love. This girl doesn't play silly games and it's just not in her to lie about anything, particularly her feelings. She's a trustworthy, loyal, and enthusiastic partner, provided she's in the right relationship.

The Aries woman wants a partner to desire her with passion and power, not some over-sensitive romantic or love-sick puppy. Nothing would turn her off quicker than a doormat for a lover. This girl will never be caught pandering to the fragile male ego. She's incredibly idealistic and wants a knight in shining armor. Only a guy who performs great feats in the world will win her heart. The Aries woman needs a partner she can look up to and feel proud of, and once she has him, she becomes his entire support network—the ultimate cheerleader. Should anybody cross or criticize her lover, she will swiftly transform herself into an avenging angel and neatly dispatch the culprit in order to defend her true love. She expects nothing less in return, so if she feels neglected or unappreciated, her partner should be ready to hear about it—and loudly!

Yes, she can be bossy, and yes, she can be jealous, demanding, and argumentative, but she does it all with a delightful naivety that is refreshingly honest and endearing. After all, she only wants her partner to be as perfect on the outside as she knows he is on the inside. She hasn't invested her precious heart in a relationship in order for it to fall short of its potential. Add that to her blatant, direct sexuality, and this girl is as attractive as she is irresistible. When it comes to expressing her love in a physical sense, no partner will be left in doubt as to the power of her feelings. She approaches lovemaking with the same ferocity as she approaches every other aspect of her life, with a single-minded vigor that is totally seductive in its vitality and passion. She makes her lover feel as though he's the only person in the world who can make her happy. She quickly learns what "does it for him" and then generously devotes herself to his pleasure. If the Aries woman feels this is reciprocated, then what happens in the bedroom is sure to be frequently repeated.

ARiES WOMAN WiTH **ARiES MAN**

In love: There's a strong initial spark of attraction between these two. After all, which Aries wouldn't love the image of him or herself? As these are two thrill-seeking people, both constantly looking for something new, it's not a case of "what shall we do?" but "what shall we do first?" This is a relationship that offers dedication and sincerity—indeed everything anyone could ever wish for. The Aries man and Aries woman think very much alike, and together these two energetic, enthusiastic people make a heady cocktail. Both will enjoy the highly charged banter, upbeat tempo, and stimulating company of someone so similar. There will never be a dull moment as they treat each aspect of their daily lives as an adventure. Neither has much time for sentimental romance since they just can't sit still long enough to gaze into each other's eyes. But there's also a nuance of fun and teenage love about this romance; it's fresh and exciting and each puts the other up on a pedestal in order to admire one another. There's enough mutual affection here to bring this relationship to marriage. No pussyfooting around, they're both forward enough to get it going. However, they'll want to explore all sides of the relationship, and, given time, this will invariably lead to the discovery that they both have very hot tempers—Yeow! Never mind the kid gloves; they'll need oven mitts to handle one another.

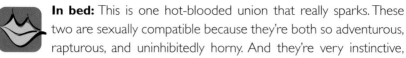 **In bed:** This is one hot-blooded union that really sparks. These two are sexually compatible because they're both so adventurous, rapturous, and uninhibitedly horny. And they're very instinctive, so seduction techniques are completely unnecessary. Since neither has the patience to play the cat-and-mouse games that are the usual prerequisites for bedroom antics, they're unlikely to recognize a subtle sexual advance anyway. When the Aries woman and Aries man get the urge, making love is wild, fast, and frenetic. It takes only an instant to get this couple going, so they'll undoubtedly be members of the mile-high club, the dressing-room club, the back seat club, the front steps club… One minute they can be having a lively conversation at home over dinner and the next, the plates are on the floor and they're on the table! They both agree that the trouble with instant gratification is that it takes too long. Sex is a very important component in their relationship and it's unlikely that they will ever go off it, or that they can do without it for very long. However, with two people who have the lowest boredom thresholds of the zodiac, the question is: How long will it be before they reach burn-out? They are both potentially dedicated people, and as long as they constantly challenge one another to keep this love alive, it could be cooking for a very long time.

ARIES WOMAN WITH **TAURUS MAN**

In love: Aries is attracted to almost anything with a pulse and the Taurus man's pulse is so strong and steady that if flashing lights were attached to him, the Aries lady would definitely be moving, grooving, and dancing to his beat. Romantically, the Taurus man will fulfill her deepest desires and offer a sense of emotional security, just as the energetic Aries lady inspires positive, pulsating action from her Bull. In order to keep this up, however, they will have to work hard. The Aries lady, coming home every day to a safe and secure environment, may find things somewhat monotonous and this may impel her to inject a new rhythm that could take him a while to get in step with. Fast on his feet this guy is not, but neither has he got two left ones. In fact, his grace of movement is deliciously appealing so long as the Aries girl doesn't fire up his temper, and then it's like putting "bull" and "china shop" together in the same life sentence. The first few weeks of this coupling should reveal all, and if they can get through the initial adjustments, they could very well go the whole distance. His calming influence on her is something that she could not only get used to, but also begin to enjoy, while the uplifting impact that the Aries female has on the Taurus man will undoubtedly make him feel more alive and keep him smiling.

 In bed: The Taurus man is romantic and will go to great lengths in order to set the mood with candles, fine wine, and luxurious surroundings. But the lady Ram may have to go against nature and slow down to enjoy the gradual build-up that the Taurus man loves to indulge in. The Taurus man may be slow but he always gets to the finish. When it comes to endurance, he takes first prize and he's unlikely to let her down. He'll find the Aries woman's passionate nature and sexual excitement stimulating but he won't expect to come to an exhausted, sweaty halt after just five minutes. He doesn't have the same level of energy as the Aries woman but he has bags more stamina. Nevertheless, they do have something in common: they are both very sexy creatures, so with her energy and his staying power, sex could be the main attraction of their relationship. However, he's a sensitive soul and doesn't take well to being strung along. He's also a stayer, so if she's unsure at the start, it would be better to stop sooner rather than later.

ARIES WOMAN WITH GEMINI MAN

In love: Aries is the first of the Fire signs and Gemini is the first of the Air signs. Together, these two make a wild combination. They'll get on like a house on fire. The Gemini man, with his eternally questing mind and quick intellect, will always have some new idea to fascinate the Ram girl, with her lightning-fast wit. There's a sense of real potential in this union. From the moment they first meet, a playful quality radiates through their relationship. They're like two children growing up together, always getting into mischief and laughing their heads off over some private joke. However, they never quite seem to reach maturity, which is great until they have to behave like grown-ups, for example in the presence of authority—bosses, parents, policemen, and so on. They could easily get themselves into trouble, but their time together will be more fun than a barrel of monkeys. They're both eternally youthful and will resist any old-fashioned ways. That's not to say that they let the serious side of life slide completely. They will get on with it: they just won't let it get them down. The Aries woman and Gemini man will make a firm bond yet will still manage to give one another some space. String-quartet romance and whispered sweet nothings are unlikely to be heard often, if at all. Instead, lively conversation and silly jokes will create a constant babble of noise.

In bed: The Aries woman is clever but so is the Gemini man and he'll have talked his way into her bed before she's even realized what's happened. Or, if she did realize, she let him do it anyway because she so enjoys the entertainment. Geminis are entertaining and unpredictable lovers, and they are rarely ever boring when they get between the sheets, which should be enough to satisfy any Aries girl's thirst for novelty. She'll be fascinated with the Gemini man's ability to flit from one pleasure zone to another, constantly surprising her with his unusual rhythms. He will adore her pure, uncompromising passion and the enthusiasm with which she responds to his artful ministrations. Geminis are known for their wandering minds, but an Aries woman won't give him the chance to think about anything else while she single-mindedly pursues the satisfaction of her sexual appetites. The only place his mind will be wandering when he's with her is in and around her body. They're a fantastic match. Gemini is great with his hands and she'll definitely let his fingers do the walking—all over her body! With his flowing energy and skillful lovemaking, he'll be the only person the Aries woman will ever wait for, while she knows exactly how to wind her Gemini man up to the point of frenzy.

ARiES WOMAN WiTH **CANCER MAN**

 In love: The Cancer man will make the most cozy, warm, and inviting home any woman could ever hope for; however, the Aries girl is far too busy to take much notice. That's not to say that all his efforts will be unappreciated; it's just that she's not the most domesticated creature in the world, and if someone else is catering to her needs in that area, then she'll return the favor by providing all sorts of spontaneous fun and excitement. "Well, that's great," says the Cancer man, "but I've just spent all day preparing the perfect romantic dinner, so do we really need to go out partying tonight?" And the Aries girl replies, "But we did the whole romantic dinner thing last week!" That's it: his feelings are hurt, she's totally at a loss to see why, and nobody ends up enjoying themselves, at least not if they spend the evening together. However, if they do have a mutual aim in life, together they can make a very strong team. They both have an ability to dive into the unknown and to give every single ounce of energy to a good cause. As long as the Cancer man doesn't make it his business to try to capture the Aries woman, this coupling could work. If she's ever feeling down, this man will give her the boost she needs; he'll hold her in his protective arms and let her know exactly where she belongs. She'll never want for comfort while she's with him. He's a clannish man and if the Aries girl is into it, she'll soon find she's been adopted into his family.

In bed: When it comes to lovemaking, or anything else for that matter, the Cancer man is tenacious. He has a gripping manner and doesn't tend to let go or to move too fast. He's also determined to be the instrument of his woman's pleasure so he won't let the Aries woman down in her demand for sexual satisfaction, though some adjustments will be necessary. The Cancer man performs best in the bedroom when there is a heavy emotional content to the proceedings. He doesn't get off on the purely animalistic. He'll do his duty of course, as he's an excellent provider, but it might just lack the passionate fervor that the Aries woman needs if she's going to want a repeat performance. And as she usually likes all-night repeats and re-runs, she had better be able to show him that she's got some depth to her feelings. She won't be able to fake it either, because he's incredibly intuitive and will immediately spot a sham. She will have to get in touch with her inner self at least during the physical part of this relationship. In return, he will reach the deep, dark depths that she would previously not have been aware of. He will make her feel cherished and emotionally secure but he's moody, so, if she still wants to give him a go, she'll need to try to ebb and flow with the Cancer ups and downs.

ARiES WOmAn WiTH **LEO MAN**

 In love: This is a seriously dramatic relationship. The Leo man has all the grandeur of a king and is someone the Aries girl can admire and be proud of. He's an exhibitionist but in the most dignified way. The Aries girl has all the childlike effervescence and naive enthusiasm necessary to bring out his enormous sense of fun as well as his protective and possessive instincts. They both love the admiration and attention they receive when out together in public, but when they are "à deux" behind closed doors, the story may, on occasion, be slightly different. He requires constant adoring attention from his mate, while she absolutely must come first in everything. If the relationship develops a strong competitive edge, a battle of wills could ensue, and with such a fiery couple, it would be hard to pick the winner. Since both are Fire signs, they deal with one another's enthusiasm, optimism, and passionate energy with deep understanding, and because there is such a degree of acceptance between them, they're able to encourage each other, even though they also know how to get to one another. The thing is, his warmth and generosity mean he's brilliant at making her feel that she's the most important person in the world, while she so single-mindedly expresses her ardor that he'll feel like royalty. This is true love where each genuinely admires the achievements of the other. They could laugh and love forever.

In bed: Feeling hot, hot, hot! As saucy goes, Tabasco has nothing on these two. Just one slightly spicy hint of sex in the air and they can barely contain their desire to take a bite out of the other's flesh—metaphorically speaking of course. They're both energetic, if not acrobatic. The sheer physical passion of this union is explosive. It's not a quiet affair. They sense each other's desires and needs and he's generous enough to grant all that she could wish for, while she knows that with her Leo, the more she gives, the more she will receive, and *nearly* as often as she wants. After all, the king of beasts does like to laze around occasionally, particularly if he's been worn out by an Aries girl. She'll still want to kiss him all over and he won't be able to keep his paws, er, hands, off her for long—especially when they are in the great outdoors, where Lions roam and Rams run free. He'll want to show her how good he can be at the hunt when he's hungry for love, and she loves to be pursued. A good chase is the perfect aphrodisiac for both these Fire signs. He'll be proud to show her that there's nothing tame about him when he's on the prowl!

ARiES WOMAN WiTH **ViRGO MAN**

In love: The Virgo man with his modest and meticulous ways holds a strange fascination for the Aries woman. She's quieter, softer, and gentler in his company—at least for a while. She can appreciate that he's a clever man, able to dispel any uncertainties that arise in her life by analyzing, prioritizing, and organizing that life into a neat package. And because he appears to magically put things in order, she finds him fascinating, even compelling. He, on the other hand, sees her as a wonderfully unspoiled project, and is impressed by her directness, honesty, and innocence(!) He looks forward to unraveling her and putting her back together in a more refined, less erratic state. But nobody, not even the love of her life, is allowed to do that. She's nobody's pet project and she will resist, but that will just make her appeal to him even more. That is, of course, unless she has unleashed her famous Aries temper. Virgo men do not like to be criticized, particularly by a wildly angry, loud, and unladylike lover. They'll both sit down, talk it through, and come to a deeper understanding, but just a little of the shine will have rubbed off. It's a relationship that offers a learning experience for both, so if they're into lessons, they'll be in for the education of a lifetime. The contrast in their personalities will teach them all they need to know about themselves as individuals.

In bed: He's born under the sign of the Virgin, but make no mistake, this isn't his first time, even though she would probably like it to be. Remember, the Aries woman wants the first bite of every cherry! Certainly, they can both pretend it's his first time every once in a while, and this will add to the excitement, but her flagrant freshness brings a sense of all that is new and untouched to every sexual encounter. The Virgo man is renowned for giving good service and works very well under direction. She, meanwhile, falls naturally into the role of leader and will be able to direct him so that he dutifully fulfills her desires. But don't get the idea that he doesn't move unless told to do so. He's no lap dog, although she wouldn't complain if he were! If he's left in charge, the Virgo man is capable of driving Ms. Aries into a flurry of delight. He'll get straight into her head for a start, and work his way down (via the heart, of course). He's subtle yet very sexual, explicit, and exacting — no part of the Aries woman will be left uncharted.

ARİES WOMAN WİTH **LİBRA MAN**

In love: This is a happy union in almost every sense. The Libra man takes a genuine interest in everything about the Aries woman and really loves her dynamic and powerful personality. The fact that she's got something to say for herself and doesn't hesitate in saying it is a real turn-on for him, and is something he could learn from her. She's impressed by his seemingly effortless charm and stimulating mind, both of which he uses to capture her attention. As opposites in the zodiac, the two of them make one whole. Each has what the other is missing. On occasion her impetuosity is a little too rash or brash for his refined taste, just as his endless deliberating and inability to make a decision can have the Aries woman tapping her foot in irritation. But the longer these two hang around each other, the more they find things to love, adore, and be thankful for in their relationship. At some point, they may really begin to meld and start taking after one another. They'll even begin to look, sound, and think alike. Finishing one another's sentences will not be a source of irritation. Instead, it will be a comfort to be so thoroughly in tune with someone else. Both enjoy the excitement of a new challenge and neither is content to sit around waiting for life to come to them. Their mutually absorbing and eternally oscillating existence brings this couple into the realms of heavenly rapture.

In bed: Nothing appeals to the libido of a Libra man more than a woman who can match him in the mental realm. The Aries woman's passionate and fiery discourse sets his pulse racing, with the result that he desires nothing more than to race her into the bedroom. She'll be delighted by the way he responds to every move she makes. The more he feels her pleasure, the more he will give himself over to the whole experience. This girl doesn't know the meaning of holding back and nor will he once she invites him in. Their lovemaking reaches the parts that other mere sexual indulgences cannot reach. In fact, he'll reach parts of her that she didn't even know she had. And all because he knows the lady loves it. His cool, refined Libra persona and her unbridled desire and passion will create a special kind of chemistry between them. Here is a man who is as restless as the Aries woman. Neither will be able to sit still for long in the company of the other, and neither will want to. This is a "rock 'n' roll" match in every sense. These two will forever be captivated by the prospect of exploring each other's depths.

ARIES WOMAN WITH **SCORPIO MAN**

In love: There's a powerful magnetic attraction between these two, a challenge that neither will be able to ignore very easily. Both signs are ruled by Mars, so the Scorpio man and the Aries woman will naturally have a shared sympathy for one another. He's all self-confidence and controlled, hidden passion, while she's all self-confidence and overt, unbridled passion. Passion is what they have in common, not just the lusty kind, but the kind that generates action and energy. The fuel that they create between them would certainly fire a rocket into space and beyond. They're a powerful pair and can easily perceive one another's fighting spirit and admire it—that is, until they're fighting with each other, which is something that can happen quite easily if these two aren't careful. Careful? An Aries woman? She can be terribly thoughtless at times, which will cut her surprisingly sensitive Scorpio man to the quick. Then heaven help her. He will let her know with stinging accuracy just how dreadfully she has behaved, and it will all escalate from there. They are both competitive but in different ways. She's the obvious up-front one, while he's discreet and devious. Most Aries girls can bounce back from anything, but she'll know never to make the same mistake twice when she's involved with a Scorpio man. If he wants to keep her, he'll need to adjust his tolerance levels to accommodate this wild woman's tactics, but much to his frustration, he'll never really possess her.

In bed: He'll think he's got her wrapped around his finger but she's far too independent to be tied down in such a restraining manner. This sexual relationship is tempestuous at best and volatile at worst. The Scorpio man has the capacity to completely enslave the Aries woman in the bedroom, and he won't give her time to think about anything other than indulging in their passionate pursuits. He is delighted not only that she can match him in physical intensity, but also that her appetite for sex is as keen as his own. Certainly, their neighbors will be aware of their carnal capers, but this won't bother either of them. They will be so into each other that nothing else matters. Scorpio is known as a manipulative sign, so she should watch how he plays her—all over. There is no doubt this is an intense and compelling union. As though she were on a mission, the Aries woman knows what she wants when it comes to sex, and so does the Scorpio man. Together they make an awesome duo that most couples can only dream of. They could end up either making love for the world or fighting to the bitter end. What this couple needs is less armor and more *amour*.

ARIES WOMAN WITH **SAGITTARIUS MAN**

 In love: These two could fall in love at first sight. It's as though they both immediately recognize the fact that they share an adventurous, questing spirit—one that puts a fire in their hearts that makes them live, love, and lust with sweet abandon. However, the Sagittarius man is known for his wandering. She will adore being his intrepid traveling companion as he wanders over her body, but if he wanders in the direction of someone else's, it's unlikely to amuse the usually game Aries woman. She demands to be his one and only! And the truth is, she has all that this man could or would ever want from a life partner. He's amazed at her willingness to face obstacles head on and at her display of resilience as she picks herself up with a smile and a wave when life has momentarily got her down. She is intrigued by the way he embraces the philosophical and the spiritual: he has the capacity to broaden her mind, feed her hungry soul, and enhance her spiritual awareness at a physical and emotional level. However, while they both enjoy a good laugh, they should tone down the energy levels and be sensitive to other people's need for peace if they want to keep their friends. Once these two make a commitment to one another, life will never be the same again, but who wants a past when there's such a bright future?

 In bed: The twinkle in his eye tells her that she's in for the ride of her life! The fire in hers lets him know that he'd better do something about it now or he'll lose her forever. They know they want one another as soon as they set eyes on each other, but this burning passion will need to be tamed or else it could rage out of all control in a very short period of time. She'll inspire him to be fast on his feet, and he'll keep her on her toes while they're both head over heels. They both laugh a lot and know how to have a good time. Everyone knows that laughter is the best medicine, but they need to be careful that they don't overdose! This is a pairing with lifelong potential but to make it last, they should pace themselves. Time is not important for either of these signs, and anything is possible when the Aries woman and Sagittarius man get passionate. Fire and fire together make an inferno of unadulterated excitement. Imagine the scene … they're at her best friend's wedding and the bride lends the Aries girl the key to her honeymoon suite so she can pop up and freshen up her makeup. The Sagittarius man, ever the opportunist, follows. Spontaneity is the name of his game.

ARIES WOMAN WITH **CAPRICORN MAN**

In love: If she is an Aries woman of a more serious persuasion, the Capricorn man will appeal to her sense of purpose and determination. Likewise, if he's the type of Goat that enjoys the occasional nudge up the mountain, he'll be very attracted by the pushy lady Ram. Both are ambitious and self-reliant, and at best, this relationship could get them where they want to go that little bit faster. However, this is unlikely to be a sumptuously romantic pairing. It's a love that needs time to mature because Capricorns are not known for their impulsive actions and, unfortunately, the Aries woman doesn't like to wait around. She knows her feelings immediately and won't take kindly to his testing each stage of the relationship to make sure it's safe to move on to the next step. She expects him to open his heart as readily as she does, but the Capricorn man is just not like that. His loyalty needs to be earned. The Capricorn man could use an Aries woman to help him to loosen up and try being spontaneous rather than planning everything, while she needs him to remind her to look before she leaps. As both are Cardinal signs, they could clash when each thinks he's right, but if they can agree to agree before disagreeing, or at least agree to disagree, they could have something very special going between them. This is not the most comfortable of relationships and it will require work, but if they're both willing to meet halfway, it could be very rewarding.

In bed: When it comes to sex, the Capricorn man is very physical and highly composed. He could move the earth for any deserving female. He's the master of self-control and discipline yet he's not one to risk a fleeting passion so the Aries woman will have to wait for him to initiate the process. There it is again! That "waiting" thing. But the Aries woman would be well advised to wait for this guy. The male Goat's passion is so coiled up inside him that once he lets go, one of the few people that could handle the intensity of his sensual ardor is an Aries. And boy will she handle him! He'll be incredibly turned on by her enthusiastic expressions of love and her sense of adventure will delight his lingering libido. But getting to this stage of the relationship might take longer than the Aries lady is willing to wait. If she is aware of what she might be missing if she doesn't wait for him, it might still work out because he offers not just a promise of satisfaction. She'll be quaking after all his deliberations. And he'll be moved, too, so the rhythm between them becomes self-perpetuating, and once they get going, there will be no stopping them!

ARIES WOMAN WITH **AQUARIUS MAN**

In love: The gregarious Aquarius man and the expressive Aries woman make for a great combination. She loves him for the way he continually comes up with fascinating facts and original ideas. He adores her independence and willingness to try anything new. They'll both be stimulated by the ever-moving flow of thought, inspiration, and information between them. They'll feed off each other and would do so literally, given the chance, but there's just one thing that might make it difficult for this relationship to move beyond devoted friendship. He appears emotionally aloof. Even if he can't get her out of his mind, the Aquarius man has a very hard time letting the Aries woman know just how deeply she affects him. He'll be lapping up her direct and ardent expressions of love, yet somehow he can't quite make the leap and declare his feelings with the same amount of fervor. He'll call her up, ask her to meet him, take her to dinner, and generally try to spend as much time in her company as possible, but he needs to be completely sure that he won't be rejected before he lets her see into his heart and the enormous amount of space she takes up there. Luckily, most Aries girls have good instincts, so she'll know without having to be told. This relationship is in no way hard work for either of them. In fact, there's no need to try at all; there is a natural love and acceptance between them, and neither will ever feel bored!

In bed: The Aquarius man is an innovative lover. Even a thrill-seeking Aries woman will be left with dropped jaw and raised eyebrows at some of his sexual suggestions. He'll love the fact that she'll never say no, and why would she? His perceptive friendliness along with his inventive and occasionally kinky sexuality makes him her ultimate turn-on. Intellectually, this man stimulates and inspires the hungry Aries woman's appetite for life, so she'll never fret for something to do or think about, in or out of bed. Her quick and agile mind ensures that he'll never be bored as long as his attention is centered on her. She is youthful, active, and equally inspiring to him, which helps to shake his detached demeanor into something that could look suspiciously like intimacy. They offer one another the freedom they both need but one great thing about the sexual relationship of an Aquarius man and an Aries woman is their total lack of inhibition. When both are satisfied, they'll happily lie around talking about some fascinating subject until the glow of dawn creeps in through the window then, rather than roll over and go to sleep, they'll be rested enough to make love all over again and until well past breakfast.

ARIES WOMAN WITH PISCES MAN

In love: The Pisces man will fulfill every fantasy of the Aries woman and he'll be whatever she wants him to be, whether that's a prince, a handyman, or a masseur. However, he requires loads of attention, appreciation, and affection in return. If she can provide these he'll be hers forever. If she can't, he may behave in one of two ways: either he'll follow her around like the lovesick puppy an Aries girl just can't abide, or he'll simply drift away and she'll never see him again. The Pisces man is fascinated by the single-minded energy with which an Aries woman approaches life. Part of him feels so connected to her, yet there is another side to him which is connected to noone and nothing or, better put, to everyone and everything. He's a chameleon-like lover and she'll be a sucker for his charm, which he possesses in bucketfuls, but she might just run for it when she grows tired of trying to figure him out. Realistically speaking, she might not possess the kind of refined qualities that he prefers a woman to have. As their signs are positioned next to one another in the zodiac, it's possible that the Aries woman and Pisces man have some planets in common and in this case, the pairing could work out beautifully. If not, they could very well make an odd couple, he being dreamy and introspective, she focused and extrovert.

 In bed: If she needs to find out what's on his mind, the Aries girl will need to sum up all her directness and she must ask in the most explicit terms, because the Pisces man can be very ambiguous. However, this man is able to create the ultimate sexual fantasy, with her in the starring role. He's into feet and she's into heads, so together they could write their own version of the Kama Sutra. He has the ability to bring out the Aries woman's secret desire to feel soft and feminine. The dreamy way he envelops her in his romantic lovemaking has her longing to play the femme fatale. Her raw desires and pure passion have him feeling like an all-powerful super sex god. There's only one slight problem, though. He wants her to be a softly sensual feminine lady, just as she needs him to be the powerful dominant man she can look up to. If things aren't working out as though they were the stars of a romantic film, he might do a vanishing act. He's an elusive guy so if the Aries woman's attention has waned and her head is turned, he'll be with someone else before she knows it. Neither will ever fully understand the other. Although these two are very different creatures, if they're happy to remain in a state of flux, their relationship could work out well, as it has some very positive things going for it.

THE **ARIES MAN** IN LOVE

The Aries male is about as male as they come. He is single-minded, bold, brave, and, in a very heartfelt way, raw, romantic, and ready for action. Not capable of wooing a woman in the traditional "champagne and roses" kind of way, he's more likely to woo her on the edge of some precipice, just before the two do a "couples" bungee jump. There's no doubt he offers a life of adventure and heart-pounding thrills. A date with the Aries man is not for the fainthearted, nor for any girl who wants a relaxing time out.

The Aries man has a lot to offer: he is industrious and resourceful, and will never leave a woman in need, so long as she is adaptable. He doesn't follow convention, because he's out there breaking new ground. There's a large element of experimentation with Aries, so what he provides will be wildly beyond all expectations, for better or worse. The woman who dares to go out with him must be able to hold his interest and present him with a challenge, a lifetime chase, yet she must also offer him absolute devotion because, although his attention will stray, he is surprisingly in control of his actions and remains impeccably loyal.

Aries is a man who would risk his life for the woman he loves. His reactions are quick, so neither an oncoming bus, nor a man-eating lion would stand in the way of a heroic Aries man in love. He is the cave man of the zodiac, wearing his heart on his sleeve, and when he meets his ideal cave woman, she'll be fighting him off as he tries to drag her away by the hair. But the truth is that he's more sophisticated than that. He's really more of a

Tarzan because his ideal is more of a Jane—clever, strong, independent, yet vulnerable to his innate masculine charm.

What's the bad news? Two things. Firstly, he has very little patience, particularly when it comes to talking about people's feelings. Long, drawn-out emotional conversations will be construed as whining. His chosen woman will be his soul mate but she will need other friends to air her feelings to because, when she does so to him, he'll only make inane suggestions such as telling her to go and have a rest while he gets on with more important things. However, his eternally uplifting spirit is enough to keep any woman high. There's really never a dull moment.

Secondly, don't make this knight in shining armor mad! His temper is explosive, but the consolation is that it is short-lived. Anyone on the receiving end of his fury needs to take cover but be able to bounce back quickly. His bedroom style is not dissimilar. It's powerful, but if marathon lovemaking sessions are what you expect, prepare to be disappointed.

ARiES mAn WiTH **ARiES WOmAn**

See pages 54–55.

ARIES MAN WITH **TAURUS WOMAN**

In love: He is the man of men. Being an Aries and ruled by Mars, he is positively and deliciously masculine, impulsive, and aggressive. He could be very protective toward the lady Bull, who, being an Earth sign ruled by the planet Venus, is the ultimate sensuously indulgent female. He'll be attracted to her immediately, without knowing why, but that won't bother him. He'll happily accept the peace and understanding that she offers. She'll be someone to wipe his weary brow and envelop him in emotional and physical luxury while he recharges his batteries. She, on the other hand, will find his boyish bravado irresistible. He brings such excitement and newness to her life. He's never boring, always active, and rarely gets under her feet. And that's where things might not always be perfect, for occasionally she likes having him around and one hundred percent there for her. She is possessive, and he doesn't take kindly to being tied down. He will always be there for her, as long as she doesn't demand his presence. In return, she will bring stability and security to his fast-paced lifestyle. The Taurus woman enjoys frequent quiet moments, when there's just the two of them together and a heavy scent of romance in the air. He, the ultimate masculine figure, will be drawn by her feminine charms and her offer of love and devotion. They might not recognize it immediately, but this couple has a lot to offer one another in the long term.

In bed: There's never a dull moment with the Aries man! He's full of surprises and this could either make the Taurus lady a little edgy or it could fill her with delightful anticipation, making her perpetually ready and willing to find out what's going to happen next. His enthusiasm can be infectious, especially if she's up for the thrills and spills that the Aries man never fails to provide. It will take time and patience on the part of the Taurus woman to get her Aries man to consider her sexual needs, since he can be a bit of a "wham-bam-thank-you-ma'am" kind of lover. She normally prefers a slower pace. But she shouldn't be too quick to judge. That's his department, being master of the quickie. Although this man might not give her all she needs first time around, he doesn't always stop with just one fleeting sexual session. When he's decided that he wants an evening of sex, he's a many-times-a-night-guy. The Taurus woman has both the stamina and the sensual allure to make sure she has her desires satisfied, and often. His raw energy is highly desirable but if she feels that he needs taming, she's certainly got the depth and the patience to do it. He may burst with eagerness while she slowly and thoroughly shows him her way, but given time, he'll learn to hold back. She'll show him what to do and he won't forget in a hurry because he'll quickly become addicted to her sensuous touch and will want to come back for more!

ARIES MAN WITH GEMINI WOMAN

In love: The witty, flirtatious, lighthearted Gemini woman draws the Aries man to her like a bee around a honeypot. She thrills to his energetic masculinity with such obvious delight that she captures and engages his fascinated attention. These two will feel an immediate infatuation with each other and the attraction is powerfully intriguing to both. The intelligent, stimulating conversations that they will indulge in will provide hours of surprise and pleasure. The initial enticement can quite naturally develop into a compelling love, provided the Gemini girl doesn't let her Aries man see her flirting with other men. It's not that she necessarily wants to attract more bees, it's just that her boredom threshold is very low, so she can't help but inject a little bit of excitement into any conversation. However, since the Aries man knows that he is exciting enough for ten women, he quite naturally won't understand. In this relationship, nothing should be taken for granted and expectations must be verbalized. When it comes to commitment, it will need to be spelled out, as both parties enjoy freedom and neither handles rejection well. Whether it lasts forever or not, this will be one of the most memorable experiences of both their lives, and they'll be grateful to have crossed each other's paths. Quantity isn't the issue here: quality is. It's possible for this well-matched couple to go the distance and enjoy the many intimacies that will grow between them as time goes on, but if one of them gives up, they can both call it quits.

In bed: The Aries man is the party that the Gemini woman has been dressing up for all her life and once they find one another, she'll be ready to strip off completely while teasing him mercilessly. There's lots of fooling with this couple! The Gemini woman is capable of making his toes curl with total ecstasy because she can touch and stimulate him intellectually like no other. She spins such a yarn, arousing his imagination and raising his blood pressure until he believes she's a goddess of love walking the earth. She sees him as her inspiring hero and can't wait to run her hands over him. They're both tactile creatures and very fast movers when it comes to sexual expression. She's Air, he's Fire —an essential combination for raising the sexual temperature — so the room may well start smoking and the fire engines may have to be called. This couple should make sure the bed is equipped with a fire blanket, and they should also check that those chandeliers are well attached to the ceiling, as they're both into variety!

ARIES MAN WITH CANCER WOMAN

In love: The Aries man arrives on the scene like a knight in shining armor and the Cancer woman is the maiden he intends to rescue. She'll think he's wonderful and there's absolutely no doubt he'll be attracted to her and will proceed to try to make everything right in her life. When the Cancer woman uses her feminine wiles and looks devotedly into the eyes of her Aries man, the flattery he feels is enough to undo him. But this man doesn't know the meaning of patience. He can't handle situations that are dripping with emotion, whereas the Cancer girl thrives on emotional energy and is very romantically inclined. Although her heart is susceptible to his heroic nature, she needs to know her man has a deep capacity for real love and powerful emotions. The Aries man does have that capacity, but he doesn't express it in a way she can always recognize. He'll love her as long as she's happy but unfortunately, he has very little patience when dealing with emotional outbursts. He will try, but however hard he tries, his efforts are unlikely to meet her standards. He's happy to go along with her other quirks — like the regular visits she makes to her family — and he might even enjoy them. She'll honestly believe she's good for him because she'll encourage him to nurture family ties. This is a love that will grow but will need assistance from friends and family.

In bed: When the Cancer woman is in the mood for sex, she'll find the Aries man definitely worth stripping down for, at least once. If she's ever emotionally overwrought and floundering in a sea of tears, he'll probably not even notice. This can actually be very helpful because she'll quickly forget her troubles once her mind and heart are focused on his hot-blooded embrace. She should think of him as a sex therapist — someone who is so passionately expressive and sexually demanding that while her body is entwined in his she'll be able to think of nothing else. He'll make her forget her tears, and possibly even the reason for them. He's fascinated by the way her changing mood can make her appear to be a different woman, yet somehow the same one he fell for. He'll be delighted at the possibility of being able to show off his bedroom prowess to an endless array of delectable females. Her multi-faceted nature will keep the Aries man happy, so she can rest assured that he won't stray. He knows how to handle her in bed, that's for sure! He's a horny devil who's ripe and ready at the slightest innuendo and he'll see the possibilities in the most mundane acts.

ARIES MAN WITH **LEO WOMAN**

In love: The Leo woman, not known for giving her heart away easily, will be generous when it's an Aries man who's captured her attention. She'll be drawn naturally to his youthful and enthusiastic temperament; however, she won't make it easy on this flashy lion-tamer. But once she sees that he's only got eyes for her and that he is, in fact, capable of offering loving devotion, she'll be surprisingly docile as long as his concentration doesn't wander. It's true that he likes a regular change of scenery, as he's very visual, but it doesn't mean that he's promiscuous. She's possessive and proud, and heaven help him if he gets distracted, even for a second. She's remarkably quick and her lioness's claws and teeth are sharp! But this woman knows how to present herself. She is usually breathtakingly beautiful and has an extravagant but refined glamor, all of which is totally irresistible to the Aries man. As far as she's concerned, his self-confidence and innate leadership are highly desirable qualities and she's impressed by his strength of character. She'll be generous with this man, not only with gifts, but also with favors, time, and most importantly, her heart. And he's very keen on showing her that she's exactly his type. Public displays of affection are not uncommon with these two but their dignity will not suffer inappropriate displays of sentimentality, so you'll never see them getting gooey-eyed in public — they keep all that to themselves.

 In bed: The Leo woman has a strong sense of drama and will easily keep the Aries man interested thanks to her role play and wide variety of costumes. There's so much mutual admiration between these two that they can have an amazing time together. This sexual union is give and take at its best, but if she ever lets him get away with it, he might just conveniently forget her turn. But the Leo lady doesn't have to make demands. He'll know when he's gone too far — and lucky for him! This lady's proud and lofty manner should have him crawling on his knees. And when they really get into the hot stuff, she'll be so taken with his ardent expression of passion that she'll bestow upon him all the delights that it is within her power to bestow and, heaven knows, the Leo woman is never lacking power. She is demonstrative and he responds. He initiates and she will pick up and carry it on, and they'll often meet one another at the finish. Her sometimes domineering style will drive him wild just as his powerfully masculine and animalistic magnetism will have her playfully inviting him to join in the sport. They may be too hot for some, but these two energetic Fire signs are the perfect combination for making the most of playful antics, ardent feelings, and a big, big love! They'll never tire of each other's bodies.

ARIES MAN WITH VIRGO WOMAN

In love: All the fire, energy, and confidence that are so apparent in the Aries man are a complete turn-on for the composed and cool Virgo lady. He gives her a real charge, whether they're out painting the town red or holed up at home together. He finds her demure femininity highly arousing. He desperately wants her approval but somehow, she never quite feels inclined to give it to him completely. She has an incredible ability to put his life in order—not that it will be appreciated. In fact, it's something he might resent, except when it comes to being able to find things he thought were lost. She'll need to be watchful for when this Ram charges with anger: he'll leave her in a crumpled heap. Much to his dismay, unless he offers a heartfelt apology, it will take her quite a while to pick herself up off the floor, and when she does, he'll be made to feel guilty. Not a sensation that the Aries man enjoys. She'll withdraw her usual selfless support and will feel completely justified in allowing the critical side of her nature to be focused solely on him. It will be extremely hard work for the Aries man to get back in the good books of this graceful lady. If she doesn't learn to forgive and forget, he might soon decide that this relationship is too big a job for him to handle.

In bed: The sexual allure of the demure Virgo woman is quite irresistible to the Aries man, who is the kind of enthusiastic lover that will have her panting for more. Yet for all his sexual energy and powers of enticement, somehow he only scratches the surface of her well-contained sexual desires. His lust for immediate and spontaneous sexual gratification doesn't often meet with this lady's approval. She can be happy with a quickie on occasion, but more often than not she wants to see diligence and dedication in her lover. He may be up for doing it more than once, but for her that means endlessly going back to the beginning and starting all over again. It's fabulous for the figure to get a good physical workout, but just as she's warmed up for the really hard stuff, he's headed for the shower and a cup of coffee. That's not to say that this sexual relationship can't work, only that it *is* work—for both of them. With the right man, the Virgo woman is sensual and earthy, and she loves to make love but there has to be loyalty and a genuine exchange of deep feelings, both of which the Aries man might offer. At worst, a Virgo woman can stick at an unsatisfactory relationship for only so long and an Aries man, not at all. At best, as quick learners, they'll be keen to learn about one another. If they can teach one another to stick around, they'll enjoy plenty of pleasure!

ARIES MAN WITH LIBRA WOMAN

In love: The Aries man and Libra lady will be attracted to each other from the first time their eyes meet across that proverbial crowded room. This fiery man will be just wild about her overtly feminine, captivating charm, and it will inspire him to show her his own special brand of charisma. She'll be completely unable to stop herself from responding to his energetic pursuit with come-hither looks. They are both social creatures, but even when they find themselves at the most exciting of parties, they'll be leading each other in a dance of prey and predator, rather than joining in the party. Who captured who first? Now, that is the question! Each would like to think that it was he who did all the chasing. After all, an Aries man is very proud of his ability to get what he goes after. But the Libra lady has the seductive techniques of a siren, and she knows it, even if she does like to play coy. Once committed, the Aries man and Libra woman have a natural ability to get each other going when the going gets tough. They'll complement each other perfectly in most situations. However, they may have different ideas of what is best for each within the relationship. Aries can be very defiant and can upset the Libra lady's need for harmony. As long as that initial spark of attraction stays alive, and both have the energy to keep it fanned, this union will last long after all others have fallen by the wayside.

 In bed: When the Aries man pushes his way into the Libra woman's bedroom, he'll find scented sheets, soft lights, and romantic music. Was this all planned? Had she laid a trap and made him think that it was all his idea to walk into it? Who cares? He'll love it. Plus, he has a fire in him that will tangle those sheets, outshine the lights, and make her feel like she's sweating at a rock concert! On her side, the Libra lady is quite talkative in the bedroom and understands the stunning effect of using sexily spoken words to encourage and excite her Aries lover. This fires up his passion even more, making him capable of eliciting countless responses from her with each touch of his capable hands. There will, however, be the odd occasion when the raw animalistic nature of his lovemaking will seem a little rough and ready for the refined tastes of this Libra lady, just as the Aries man will feel that it's a bit of a nuisance waiting for her to set the scene for sex and seduction when he just wants to get on with it. She's too polite to object, but after he had praised her gorgeous, delectable body, it would have been more respectful of him to have seductively removed her pristine silk lingerie first.

ARIES MAN WITH SCORPIO WOMAN

In love: With two such powerfully willful people it's very easy to see why this is such a volatile relationship. Tempers flare, passions rise, and the way the Scorpio woman and Aries man affect each other is positively explosive! For them it's like living on a knife edge suspended over a raging sea. She will love his strong sense of self, his confidence, and his go-get-'em attitude to life, just as he will adore her seductive femininity and admire the way she keeps her powerful emotions under strict control. There's definitely a pull between them and they can certainly feel it! They are both passionate and energetic, but in very different ways. She is a more serious, intense, and brooding type, and she will not tolerate infantile behavior, even when it is accompanied by the sort of cheery innocence Aries is prone to. If her anger rains down on his head, he'll flare up and raise the temperature to boiling point. The trouble is that when the matter has died down, he'll be happy to forgive and forget, but the super-sensitive Scorpio woman will remember every jibe and insult, and if she hasn't made him pay for it this time, he can be sure that she'll find a way to extract every last penance in the future. In the end, although this relationship can be exciting, it could all get a bit too much for both of them and her desire to get right to the bottom of this man could be thwarted by his warrior-like resistance.

 In bed: Put your seatbelt on and get ready for the ride of a lifetime! There's an excitingly erotic and dangerous charge to the sexual relationship of the Scorpio woman and Aries man. Hot, heavy, steamy passion, is the only way to describe what happens when these two get between the sheets. They wanted sex? Well, they got it! But if this keeps going, they'll probably burn each other out. It's certainly one way to meet the challenge of a Scorpio/Aries relationship. The problem is that she has a need to achieve a deeper sexual intimacy than she's likely to get from the Ram man, and even though he's a Ram in all senses of the word, he doesn't have the patience or the inclination for being deep and meaningful on every level all of the time. For both the Aries man and the Scorpio woman, this is one combination that must be tried just once. It's too good to miss! Their combined energy output is sure to take both of these Mars-ruled signs right up to their personal limits. But be warned: the intensity of the fire between them is tangible and both could end up sore in the most unexpected of places. Muscles they never knew they had will suddenly be put to good use. They'll have a mind-blowing experience that's sure to leave them both very different from before they met.

ARiES MAN WiTH **SAGiTTARiUS WOMAN**

In love: The Aries man will respond perfectly to the Sagittarius woman's infectious optimism. These two lovers will probably always be rushing around town, having fun here, thrills there. It would be a wonder if they ever had the time to stop and look dreamily into each other's eyes. Forget dreamy. This is fiery hot and scorching with sex appeal. They have so much in common and both are passionate about life. They want to experience everything and go everywhere, and they'll just love being able to do it together. If they really "click," they'll also be able to coordinate their need to be on their own so that no time is wasted when they are apart. However, life together could get so hectic that they constantly brush problems under the carpet and end up tripping over the bumps. But that's hardly a reason not to be together. There is far more in common between these two than not, and any dating agency would naturally put them together because they are so similar in their aims. Their mutual, insatiable sense of adventure will never be exhausted, so long as they both shall live. Romance may not be of the traditional kind, but there will be no less love between these two passionate Fire signs than there is between any lovestruck pair. They just have a different way of showing it, but they both know it's there, even when they're fighting. And that's not such an uncommon occurrence as they also love to make up!

In bed: This is a gluttonous combination of delights — a serious pleasure-fest involving the love-hungry Aries man meeting the Sagittarius woman with her huge appetite for enjoyment. Just one piece of advice: a round of lovemaking between these two could last a long time, so with all the sweating they'll be doing while exploring each other's pleasure zones, they'll need to drink plenty of water. And while they're in the kitchen filling the water pitcher, they should grab the whipped cream, some honey, a few grapes, pomegranate seeds, asparagus, and oysters, and make it a real feast! And once the relationship gets started, they can both cancel their gym memberships. They'll never need to go to the gym again because they'll get the best workout possible right there in bed! The Aries man is an exciting lover, open to anything, and he won't be able to get enough of his Sagittarius temptress. There's just so much to try out, and after the food, her flair for foreign trends could see her belly dancing, acting the demure geisha, or performing the can-can, all of which will drive him mad with anticipation. She will love his attention and he'll be totally immersed in her vision and variety. She's generous to a fault and he'll very quickly learn to give as good as he gets. He has the energy and initiative needed to keep her quivering with excitement. They won't want to let each other go, and there's really no need. Between them there will be nothing but their big hearts.

ARIES MAN WITH **CAPRICORN WOMAN**

In love: Despite the Capricorn woman's usual patience in getting to know a romantic partner, there's a sense of urgency about this relationship that's fired by a need to get together quickly. Aries and Capricorn are people of action and they will waste no time finding out if it's a "yes" or a "no." One minute they're meeting each other for the first time, and the next they're ripping the clothes off each other's bodies in an attempt to understand the extraordinary attraction. If this union is to last, they need to make a conscious choice to work toward the same aims and to do all they can to keep the channels of communication wide open. As they're both busy people, they'll need to set aside time to meet. This relationship could prove to be a really amazing coalition, but while they both battle against their egos, it might be that someone else comes along and proves that life doesn't have to be so hard. The energy and compulsion to be together is certainly there, and will probably never die, but whether they will be able to make it work to their mutual benefit is another thing entirely. Both Aries and Capricorn are sincere and capable of being truly dedicated people, but if they are not basically compatible, the relationship could end up being a painful one. Both do, however, have good instincts, so they should be able to know whether this partnership is for keeps or just for fun.

In bed: Aries man's driving force is remarkable. Afterward, the Capricorn woman will be asking herself, "Did that really happen?" Then, with a wicked smile on her face, she'll be asking her amazing Aries man, "Can we please do that again? I kinda missed it the first time." Fast and furious, hot and hurried. Will these two ever slow down? If the Capricorn woman fancies a quickie because she's busy and running late for an appointment, the Aries man will give it to her every time, and as often as she likes. And she is very unlikely ever to refuse his advances simply because there is so much pleasure involved in being with this very horny man. When both are craving some pure, unadulterated pleasure, they'll always be there for one another. This is the kind of relationship that will be deep, meaningful, torrid, and sexy, or just plain old convenient. Either way, neither will lose out. On the contrary, both will gain something amazing from each and every sexual encounter. They'll both find it compelling and each will initiate the act as often as the other. If intimacy grows and love abounds, this could be a very workable match, but if the love turns stale, it could be more like hard work for both and they would be better off quitting while they're ahead.

ARiES mAN WiTH **AQUARiUS WOmAN**

In love: From the moment the gaze of the Aquarius woman falls on the Aries man, she wants him. She's intuitive about these things and while it's actually rare for an Aquarius woman to be deliberately seductive, in this case, the Aries man brings it out in her and she'll make the most of it. His energy is addictive and hers will simply electrify him. Both have an insatiable curiosity about one another and will not stop in their quest to completely uncover the other's mystique, which, of course, they'll never fully be able to do, so the curiosity just goes on and on and on. In the simplest terms, the combination of Aries man and Aquarius woman is magnetic. There's a huge charge between them that's almost tangible and that can draw them right into one another, for good. Prying them apart would be too big a challenge for any interfering female, so she shouldn't even try. But another possibility is that the high-voltage energy between the Aries man and the Aquarius woman can sometimes result in furious anger, which seems to blow up out of nowhere and which isn't fun for either of them. There is a slight possibility that this relationship could burn itself up, but the pros vastly outweigh the cons, so it's certainly worth taking the risk. This relationship has all the ingredients for a grand passion. There's nothing small about this love, and big love just grows and grows. Before they know it, they'll be an item.

In bed: This truly is a beautifully honest and sexually energetic combination. The Aquarius woman loves the way that she can have her Aries man hungry with desire and ready for some bed action whenever she wants. It's like having a man permanently at her disposal: all she has to do is say "now." He's not only happy to oblige — he can't wait. The Aries man and Aquarius woman are fast, furious, and frequent visitors to the bedroom. And that's not the only place they'll get it on; these two are innovative and kinky. It would have been a couple like Aries man and Aquarius woman who first did it in an airplane or first used sex toys. But whether they are home alone or out on the town, she won't be able to stop herself from reaching for him and he for her. He loves the spontaneity of it all and the possibility of being seen will challenge his daring and perhaps bring out his more dastardly side. All of which will, of course, really turn on that Aquarius woman. They'll both get so excited at the sheer audacity of being naughty that they might decide to try doing it in broad daylight in public. Hopefully not, however. As they're both thinkers, they'll realize that this will mean trouble and probably an end to their animal antics.

ARİES MAN WİTH **PİSCES WOMAN**

In love: The attraction between the fiery Aries man and the fairytale Piscean princess is tangible. He is flattered to his chivalrous masculine core by her initial submissiveness, which isn't all that it appears, but he'll want to see it that way. His energy just carries her along and she's happy to go with his flow—at first. It's thrilling, passionate, and inspiring for both of them to be traveling along this idealized path, but if they stay on that journey for very long, they'll realize that it cannot be sustained. Idealism must make way for reality otherwise she will have no say in where they're going and he'll be terribly disappointed when he turns around one day to find that she has vanished. Communication is a key issue between these two and if they can successfully convey their feelings and expectations to one another, they might just have a match made in heaven. The Aries man is so masculine and the Pisces woman so feminine that it's easy to see why these two feel so right together. And besides, the sex is great! But he may not be able to value her more elusive and imaginative qualities and every once in a while, he'll trample on her delicate feelings, forcing her to withdraw and become even more remote. But there is hope, and it's worth persevering, especially if he makes an effort to develop a little more sensitivity and if she tries to let things roll off her more readily. This could be a long-lasting relationship, but compromise is certainly needed.

 In bed: He's hot, she's ready, and together this makes one steamy love affair. Sexuality is one aspect of the relationship that could keep them together long after other connections have dwindled away. They may no longer be speaking to one another, but that won't get in the way of a good romp. They can whip each other up into a sweaty frenzy, which is so sexy and satisfying that both are left literally breathless and stunned by the awesome pleasure they've experienced. She will intuitively push the right buttons on him, and his instinctive drive will propel her straight into that ethereal realm of ecstatic bliss. One thing to realize, though, is that the Pisces woman might not be entirely present. She is certainly there in body, and is capable of going through exactly the right motions to make herself his ideal bedmate. But her soul exists on another plane and her mind could simply be elsewhere. The truth is that the reason why she so enjoys herself and loses herself so completely in the sexual act is because while she's doing it, there's a parallel world going on inside her head where she imagines the perfect lovemaking. The Aries man will be there to bring this parallel world into the real one, but if she thinks for one moment that his passion doesn't truly reflect his deeper emotions, the whole fantasy will probably come to an end. Trust is a key ingredient. Without it, she'll withhold everything she would otherwise wholeheartedly share with him.